Kylian Mbappe Lottin

A biography on Kylian Mbappe Lottin

Bollam Anirudh Krishnaa

pencil

ISBN 978-93-6263-495-5

Published in India 2026 by Pencil

A brand of
One Point Six Technologies Pvt. Ltd.
Unit no. 26, Ground Floor, Building A1,
Wadala Truck Terminal Road,
Near Post Office, Antop Hill, Mumbai - 400037
E connect@thepencilapp.com
W www.thepencilapp.com

Author biography

Hello readers,

I am Bollam Anirudh Krishnaa, and I am delighted to present everyone my first ever book, "Kylian Mbappe Lottin", I've been a football fan for the last 4 years, so I've decided to write a book on my idol, the man,the myth,the legend himself, Kylian Mbappe. I find interest in reading and writing books,and my inspiration to start writing books was Jane Austen.I am publishing this book at a ripe age of 13.I have always found interest in reading books, but recently I have also found pleaure in writing books. My special thanks goes to all my friends and classmates who have supported me through the journey, and I would like to thank my parents and my sister, who have showed me the right path of becoming a book writer.My favourite club is FC Barcelona and my favourite player is Kylian Mbappe Lottin.Visca Barca! Visca Catalunya!

CONTENTS

Chapter 1-The Legend in the Making

In December 2022, the world was watching the World Cup Final in Qatar. France was playing against Argentina, and for most of the match, Argentina looked stronger. But one player refused to give up, Kylian Mbappé.

At just 23 years old, Mbappé showed the world why he was special. He scored three goals in the final including an amazing half-volley completing his hattrick, something no player had done in more than fifty years. Even though France lost on penalties, the night belonged to him. Millions of people realized they were watching not just a good footballer, but a true superstar.

Chapter-1 (Part-2)

That moment was not the beginning of his story. It was only another step in a journey that had started many years before, in a town called Bondy, near Paris. Mbappé did not grow up rich or famous. He was simply a boy with big dreams, a football at his feet, and the support of his family. Mbappé is not only a football player, he is also an inspiration. His story shows that even if you come from a small place, you can reach the very top if you believe in yourself and keep pushing forward.

It is the story of how a shy boy with posters of Cristiano Ronaldo on his wall becomes a World Cup winner.

Chapter 2- First Steps in Football AS Bondy

When Kylian Mbappé was old enough to play in an organized team, his father took him to AS Bondy, the local football club.

At AS Bondy, Kylian trained under his father, who was one of the youth coaches. His father was strict but fair. He treated Kylian like every other player, sometimes even harder, because he wanted his son to grow with discipline. Kylian learned that talent was not enough, he had to work harder than everyone else.

He was faster than other children, and when he dribbled with the ball. He had sharp control, and he always seemed to know what to do next. Even at six or seven years old, he could run past older boys and score with ease.

But Kylian was not only a skilled player, he was also confident. He often told his teammates that he would one day play for the French national team. While many laughed, those who saw him play started to believe it could actually happen.

Outside the pitch, Kylian spent hours watching football on television. His favourite player, Cristiano Ronaldo, was his hero. He copied Ronaldo's step-overs, free-kick postures, and even his celebrations.

AS Bondy was his training ground, his home, and the place where his dreams began to look real.

Chapter 2 (Part-2)

But Kylian was not only a skilled player, he was also confident. He often told his teammates that he would one day play for the French national team. While many laughed, those who saw him play started to believe it could actually happen.

Outside the pitch, Kylian spent hours watching football on television. His favourite player, Cristiano Ronaldo, was his hero. He copied Ronaldo's step-overs, free-kick postures, and even his celebrations.

AS Bondy was his training ground, his home, and the place where his dreams began to look real.

Chapter 3-Clairefontaine Academy

As Kylian Mbappé grew older scouts from all over France had already noticed him. Some even believed he was the best young player they had ever seen at his age. His next step was clear, he needed to train at the highest level.

In 2011, at just 13 years old, Kylian was accepted into the famous Clairefontaine Academy. Great players had trained there before him, including Thierry Henry.

The best young talents from across France came together, each dreaming of becoming a professional footballer. But even among them, Kylian stood out. Coaches were amazed by his speed, dribbling, and confidence.

During matches at Clairefontaine, he often looked unstoppable.

Chapter-3(Part-2)

He could change a game on his own, dribbling past defenders and scoring goals with calm finishing. Some coaches compared him to Thierry Henry.

At this time, big clubs began to call. Chelsea, Liverpool, and even Real Madrid invited him for trials. In Madrid, he trained with the youth academy and even met Cristiano Ronaldo, his idol. But his family wanted him to grow step by step, without rushing.

Clairefontaine gave Kylian discipline, focus, and exposure. He learned how to handle pressure, how to deal with attention, and how to think like a professional footballer.

The boy from Bondy was no longer just a local talent. He was now known across France as the future of French football.

Chapter 4-Joining AS Monaco

After his time at Clairefontaine, Kylian Mbappé had many choices. Big clubs across Europe wanted him, but his family believed he should stay in France to grow carefully. In 2013 he joined the youth academy of AS Monaco, a club famous for developing young talent.

Moving to Monaco meant leaving home and living away from his family, but Kylian was determined. He wanted to become a professional footballer, and Monaco gave him the perfect platform.

Chapter-4(Part-2)

Coaches admired his focus and maturity. He trained harder than most players his age and always asked questions about how to improve.

On 2 December 2015, Mbappé made his professional debut for Monaco in a Ligue 1 match. At just 16 years, he became the youngest player ever to play for Monaco, breaking a record previously held by Thierry Henry

Chapter 5-First Professional Goal

Kylian Mbappé did not have to wait long to make history again. After becoming the youngest player ever to debut for Monaco, he was now ready to score his first professional goal.

In 2016, Monaco played against a small club in Ligue 1. The match was almost over when, in extra time, Mbappé found himself in the right place at the right time.

At just 17 years, he became Monaco's youngest-ever goalscorer, breaking a record set by Thierry Henry almost 2 decades earlier.

For Mbappé, the goal meant more than just a record. It was proof that he belonged at the highest level. His teammates celebrated with him, and his coach knew he had something special in his hands.

He began to play with even more freedom, using his incredible speed, quick feet, and intelligence to trouble defenders.

The football world was starting to take notice. Newspapers in France wrote about "the new Henry." Scouts from Europe's biggest clubs kept a close eye on him.

Chapter-5(Part-2)

For Mbappé, the goal meant more than just a record. It was proof that he belonged at the highest level. His teammates celebrated with him, and his coach knew he had something special in his hands.

He began to play with even more freedom, using his incredible speed, quick feet, and intelligence to trouble defenders.

The football world was starting to take notice. Newspapers in France wrote about "the new Henry." Scouts from Europe's biggest clubs kept a close eye on him.

Chapter 6-The Big Move to Paris Saint-Germain

Every big club in Europe wanted him, but the decision he made shocked many. Instead of moving abroad, he chose to stay in France joining Paris Saint Germain.

In2017, PSG announced the transfer. At first, it was a loan deal, but with an agreement to buy him for 180 million euros the following year. This made him the second-most expensive player in history, only behind Neymar, who had also just joined PSG from Barcelona for 222 million euros

.

At PSG, Mbappé teamed up with Neymar and Cavani to form one of the most feared attacking trios in the world.

Mbappé also settled into life in Paris with maturity. Despite all the fame and money, he stayed humble. He remembered his roots in Bondy and often visited his old neighbourhood to inspire kids.

Chapter-6(Part-2)

At PSG, Mbappé teamed up with Neymar and Cavani to form one of the most feared attacking trios in the world. Mbappé also settled into life in Paris with maturity. Despite all the fame and money, he stayed humble. He remembered his roots in Bondy and often visited his old neighbourhood to inspire kids.

Chapter 7-First Season Glory at PSG

Kylian Mbappé's first season at Paris Saint-Germain was the beginning of something special.

In Ligue 1, he continued where he had left off with Monaco. His speed terrified defenders, and his link-up play with Neymar and Cavani made PSG almost unstoppable.

That year, PSG won a domestic treble. For Mbappé, it was proof that his move to Paris had been the right choice.

One of his most memorable early PSG moments came in the Champions League against Bayern Munich. He scored and assisted in a famous 3–0 win, showing that he could shine against Europe's biggest clubs.

Chapter-7(Part-2)

But what impressed fans and experts the most wasn't just his goals—it was his attitude. Despite all the pressure of being one of the most expensive players ever, Mbappé played with joy and freedom. He celebrated every goal with passion and always gave credit to his teammates.

By the end of his first season in Paris, there was no doubt: Mbappé was more than just a rising star. He was already one of the best forwards in the world. His biggest stage was still waiting, the 2018 FIFA World Cup.

Chapter 8-The 2018 World Cup
A Star is Born

The summer of 2018 changed Kylian Mbappé's life forever. He was selected to represent France at the FIFA World Cup in Russia. Many wondered if the teenager could handle the pressure of the world's biggest tournament. Mbappé didn't just handle it he shined like never before.

In the group stage, he scored his first World Cup goal against Peru, becoming the youngest French goalscorer in World Cup history. But it was in the Round of 16 against Argentina that he announced himself to the world.

He won a penalty, then scored two brilliant goals as France won 4–3. The whole world was talking about him.

Chapter-8 (Part-2)

In the final against Croatia, Mbappé once again made history. He scored from outside the box. France won 4–2, lifting their second World Cup trophy.

Mbappé finished the tournament with 4 goals and was awarded the FIFA World Cup Best Young Player Award. More importantly, he became a global superstar.

When France returned home, millions of fans filled the streets of Paris to celebrate. Among the heroes was the teenager, now a World Cup winner.

Chapter 9-Chasing Champions League Glory

After the World Cup, Kylian Mbappé's biggest mission at Paris Saint-Germain was to win the Champions League.

In the 2019–20 season, Mbappé came closer than ever. Alongside Neymar and new teammate Di María, he led PSG on a historic run.

Then came the quarter final against Atalanta. PSG were leading 1–0 until the final minutes. Mbappé, who had just returned from injury, came off the bench and changed everything. His pace tore apart Atalanta's defence, and PSG scored two late goals to win 2–1.

PSG made it all the way to the final in Lisbon, facing Bayern Munich.

Chapter-9 (Part-2)

It was the club's first-ever Champions League final, and Mbappé had the chance to make history. He had one golden opportunity in the first half but shot straight at the goalkeeper, Neuer. Bayern eventually won 1–0, and PSG's dream slipped away.

He had carried PSG so far, but the ultimate prize was still out of reach.

Even though PSG didn't win, that season proved that Mbappé was ready for the highest level. He wasn't just a domestic star anymore, he was one of the best players in the world, capable of leading his team to the biggest stage in football.

Chapter 10-The 2022 World Cup
A Battle with Destiny

In November 2022, the world turned its eyes to Qatar for the FIFA World Cup. For Kylian Mbappé, this was more than just another tournament, it was a chance to defend France's title and prove he was not only the future of football, but also its present.

From the very start, Mbappé was unstoppable. In the group stage, he scored against Australia and twice against Denmark, securing France's place in the knockouts. His speed, sharp dribbling, and finishing made him the most feared attacker of the tournament.

In the Round of 16 against Poland, Mbappé delivered a masterclass. He scored two stunning goals, showing power and precision that no goalkeeper could stop.

France marched on, beating England in the quarter-final and Morocco in the semi-final. Mbappé wasn't always the scorer, but his presence created chaos for defences. Once again, just like 2018, he had led France to the final, this time against Argentina.

The final on 18 December 2022 turned into one of the greatest matches in football history. For 80 minutes, Argentina dominated, leading 2–0. Mbappé was quiet, almost invisible.

First, he scored a penalty to make it 2–1. Then, almost immediately after, he volleyed in a brilliant second goal to make it 2–2. France had come back from nowhere, and Mbappé was the hero.

In extra time, Argentina took the lead again through Messi, but Mbappé refused to give up. He won another penalty and calmly scored, completing his hat trick, only the second hat-trick ever in a World Cup final.

The match went to penalties. Mbappé scored his, but Argentina triumphed 4–2. France lost, but Mbappé had made history. He won the Golden Boot with 8 goals, including a final performance that will be remembered forever.

Though Argentina lifted the trophy, the night belonged to both Messi and Mbappé, one a legend completing his story, the other proving he was ready to take the crown for the future.

The world realized something that night,Mbappé wasn't just a young prodigy anymore. He was a warrior, a leader, and the man who could carry France for the next decade.

Chapter-10 (Part-2)

In extra time, Argentina took the lead again through Messi, but Mbappé refused to give up. He won another penalty and calmly scored, completing his hat trick, only the second hat-trick ever in a World Cup final.

The match went to penalties. Mbappé scored his, but Argentina triumphed 4–2. France lost, but Mbappé had made history. He won the Golden Boot with 8 goals, including a final performance that will be remembered forever.

Though Argentina lifted the trophy, the night belonged to both Messi and Mbappé, one a legend completing his story, the other proving he was ready to take the crown for the future.

The world realized something that night,Mbappé wasn't just a young prodigy anymore. He was a warrior, a leader, and the man who could carry France for the next decade.

Chapter 11-After Qatar

Though France had lost the World Cup final, Kylian Mbappé returned from Qatar 2022 as a global superstar. Scoring a hat-trick in a World Cup final and winning the Golden Boot made him the talk of the football world. For many, he was now the heir to Messi and Ronaldo.

Back at Paris Saint-Germain, Mbappé wasted no time.

The 2022–23 season, however, was full of challenges. PSG had Messi, Neymar, and Mbappé, the most feared attack in football. But off the field, rumours of tension grew. Reports said Mbappé wanted more influence in the club, and critics questioned whether the three superstars could truly play together.

Despite the noise, Mbappé kept scoring. He finished as Ligue 1's top scorer yet again, proving his consistency. But in the Champions League, PSG's dream ended early, knocked out. Once again, Europe's biggest trophy slipped away.

Chapter-11 (Part-2)

Meanwhile, Mbappé's future became the subject of endless speculation. Would he finally join Real Madrid, the club he loved as a boy? Or would he continue to lead PSG, his hometown team? Each summer, the world waited for his decision.

By 2023, one thing was clear, Mbappé wasn't just one of the best footballers, he was the face of the next generation. Because at just 24 years old, Kylian Mbappé's story was far from finished, it was only entering its most powerful chapters.

And perhaps the most inspiring part of all is this was if Kylian Mbappé could rise from the streets of Bondy to the top of world football, then every child with a dream has the power to follow their own path to greatness.

The book of Kylian Mbappé is still open. The best chapters may be yet to come.

Gist of the story

Kylian Mbappé's biography is the remarkable journey of a boy who transformed raw talent and childhood dreams into global football greatness. Born in Bondy, a suburb of Paris, Mbappé grew up in a sports-oriented family that nurtured his passion for the game from a very young age. What began as joyful kicks on local playgrounds soon revealed itself to be something extraordinary. With lightning speed, sharp intelligence, and unwavering determination, Mbappé rapidly progressed through youth academies, most notably the prestigious Clairefontaine academy, where his potential became impossible to ignore.

His professional breakthrough came with AS Monaco, where, as a teenager, he stunned the football world with his maturity, composure, and goal-scoring ability. He played a crucial role in Monaco's Ligue 1 triumph and their impressive Champions League run, announcing himself as one of football's brightest young stars. His record-breaking move to Paris Saint-Germain elevated him further into the global spotlight, where he consistently delivered breathtaking performances, collected major trophies, and formed part of one of the most feared attacking lineups in modern football.

On the international stage, Mbappé's impact was even more historic. His electrifying performances for France, especially in the FIFA World Cup, showcased not just his talent but his big-match mentality. At an age when most players are still developing, he had already etched his name into football history, earning admiration from fans, legends, and critics around the world.

Yet, Mbappé's story is not merely about goals, speed, or trophies. It is a powerful narrative of discipline, resilience, and belief. It highlights how strong family support, relentless hard work, and fearless ambition can propel a young dreamer from modest beginnings to the summit of world sport. His journey continues to inspire millions of young athletes who dare to dream beyond their circumstances.

In essence, the life of Kylian Mbappé is a modern football fairy tale — one that proves greatness is born from passion, perseverance, and the courage to chase impossible dreams.

Achievements

Club Trophies
AS Monaco

Ligue 1: 2016–17

Paris Saint-Germain (PSG)

Ligue 1: 2017–18, 2018–19, 2019–20, 2021–22, 2022–23

Coupe de France: 2017–18, 2019–20, 2020–21

Coupe de la Ligue: 2017–18, 2019–20

Trophée des Champions: 2019, 2020, 2022, 2023

International Trophies (France)

FIFA World Cup: 2018

UEFA Nations League: 2020–21

Major Individual Awards

Ligue 1 Player of the Year: 2018–19, 2020–21, 2021–22, 2022–23

Ligue 1 Top Scorer: 2018–19, 2019–20, 2020–21, 2021–22, 2022–23

FIFA World Cup Best Young Player: 2018

FIFA World Cup Golden Boot: 2022

French Player of the Year: 2018, 2019, 2022, 2023

Ballon D'or Nominations

2017 — 7th place

2018 — 4th place

2019 — 6th place

2021 — 9th place

2022 — 6th place

2023 — 3rd place
2024 — 6th place

Greatest moments in Mbappe's life

1. World Cup Breakthrough (2018)

At just 19, Mbappé lit up the 2018 FIFA World Cup in Russia. His explosive performance against Argentina in the Round of 16 stunned the world, and he later scored in the final against Croatia. France won the World Cup, and Mbappé was named Best Young Player, becoming only the second teenager after Pelé to score in a World Cup final.

2. AS Monaco Sensation Season (2016–17)

Mbappé's breakout season with AS Monaco announced his arrival to the football world. He helped Monaco win Ligue 1 and reach the Champions League semi-finals, becoming one of the most wanted young players in Europe almost overnight.

3. Record Move to Paris Saint-Germain (2017)

His transfer to Paris Saint-Germain was one of the most expensive in football history for a teenager. At PSG, he quickly became the club's main superstar, winning multiple league titles and breaking scoring records.

Greatest moments-2

4. World Cup Golden Boot (2022)
Despite France losing the final to Argentina, Mbappé produced one of the greatest individual World Cup performances ever. He scored a historic hat-trick in the final and won the Golden Boot with 8 goals ,earning worldwide admiration.

5. Becoming PSG's All-Time Top Scorer (2023)
In 2023, Mbappé surpassed Edinson Cavani to become PSG's all-time leading goal scorer, cementing his legacy as one of the club's greatest players ever.

6. UEFA Nations League Triumph (2021)